YOU START THE BUSINESS
THIS RUNS THE BUSINESS

THE BUSINESS OPERATING SYSTEM

TOM HENNESSY

2023

First Edition: 2023

ISBN 979-8-88896-079-0

Tom Hennessy Publishing

320 E. Main St.

Montrose, CO 81432

ALSO BY TOM HENNESSY

Frankenbrew - Build A Brewery For Under $20,000 (DVD)

Fabjob - Guide To Become A Coffee House Owner

Fabjob - Guide To Become A Restaurant Owner

Brewery Operations Manual:
3 Steps To Open And Run A Successful Brewery

Colorado Boy Brewery S.O.P Standard Operating Procedures
The Affordable Brewery

To Sandy,
from where all good things come from

CONTENTS

INTRODUCTION

Ten thousand. I want you to remember that number. According to the most recent (2023) Census Bureau data, taking an average over the last 5 years, 4 million businesses have been started each year. That is actually over 10,000 per day. That number is low because of the pandemic, and in fact is now growing.

Think of it, 10,000 new businesses started every single day in America. I'm sure a chunk of them are businesses on paper to move assets or whatever, but the majority are actual businesses where real people are putting their fortunes and sweat up to fulfill a dream.

Of those 10,000 roughly 50% will fail within the first 5 years. That's not because they are not good businesses, though some certainly aren't. What happens to many is the entrepreneur who started the business gets burnt out. Day in and day out dealing with all the problems of running your own business. There are so many details it just gets overwhelming.

But ask yourself this. How is it that there are national chains in your town that seem to do so well when your products are better?

Hey, they aren't even owner operated. Is it all marketing or is there something else going on?

There is no magic bullet to business success. It does take a good product, a decent location, and great marketing. There is one thing that these national chains have that you do not. A Business Operating System.

You see, it's the business operating system that actually runs the business. You manage the operating system.

I want to give you something that you can use if you are either in business or planning on starting a business. This is not a get rich quick key to success. What this little book is about is plugging this operating system into your existing business or the one you are planning.

I wish I would have had this when I started out in business when I was 29.

My two best friends and I were finally ready to open our first restaurant. We had plenty of experience, having worked our way up from dish washers to managers in large successful restaurants. We wanted to do our own thing however and struck out on our own.

At 23 I had already become the general manager of a restaurant doing a million dollars per year and had 75 employees. I worked crazy hours but enjoyed the work and the people I worked with. Becoming a general manager at 23 was my first real lesson in management, and not a good one. That lesson is called **Management by Abdication**, where the owner rather than have an experienced person run their business, just puts a warm body into the position and hopes they take care of things. I was that warm body. This was great for me as I got to learn on the job, but I don't think it was such great deal for the owner.

Back to our first restaurant. Even though we had been running restaurants, we really didn't know how to operate them from the ground up, which includes all the small details of being the owner.

Our first day went gang busters and our inexperience really showed the following morning when we took the bank bag of the previous day's receipts and dumped it all onto a table in the dining room. Now what?

We made up a Daily Sales Report (DSR) right there with a pencil and a yellow legal tablet. The old Micros cash register at least divided the sales into Food, Beverage, Wine, Beer, and sales tax. So, we wrote those down on the sheet.

Next, we counted the cash, wrote that down, then a few checks, and finally the credit card total. That was added up and balanced against what the Micros said we should have. It was within the margin of error, which we put down as Over/Short. That was our first day and the beginning of our adventure in building an operating system.

One thing became clear in the first six months of being open. The three of us were young, very enthusiastic, and not bad looking. Our customers started calling us "The Boys". I was starting to see some red flags however.

Everything that needed to be done in our business, the three of us took care of, driven by our newness and energy. But this was not sustainable. Sooner or later the burn-out factor would come into play. Or a partner might feel that he was shouldering most of the workload compared to his partners, which would create bad feelings.

Also, we had plans to grow and would want to do a second restaurant in a year or two. There were plenty of stories of businesses that grew but neglected their first business and customers would complain that it just wasn't the same as when "The Boys" ran it.

I knew even back then, that to last for the long term, the business had to stand up on its own, and not be based on just our personalities.

And so began the journey to build a business operating system.

I began by reading business books, which is what most people new to business do. There are a lot of business books out there! The one that became my lightbulb moment was called The E-Myth, by Michael E. Gerber. The basic premise of this book is that there is a myth that a successful business is run by the entrepreneur whose leadership and vision is what makes a company. He calls that a myth and what makes a business function is not the entrepreneur's vision as much as it is the systems set up to actually run the business in a consistent manner.

In one section of the book, he talked about a motel he would stay at on the California coast. It was run so well that he wanted to meet the owner to ask him (he was told it was a he) how he did it. Instead, he found a young general manager who said he simply had an operating manual that was a series of checklists that he followed to make the motel function as a smooth operating machine.

Voila! Checklists became my mantra. But I quickly found out you can't just make a bunch of checklists and expect people to actually do them. You need a system that involves checklists but is a complete and integrated system. Checklists are just one part of that system.

When I looked around at other successful businesses, they all seemed to have something internal that made them run. I compared the big successful national businesses to the small mom and pop businesses in our town. The difference was blaring. While in many cases it seemed to me that the quality of what was offered was really good at the mom-and-pop businesses, but the overall presentation was hap hazard. In the national chains the quality was more middle of the road but the way the stores were operated was spot-on. They were clean, well lit, and very consistent in their customer service. The mom-and-pop places felt like they were just hanging on.

I thought that if you had the quality of a small independent business combined with the business systems of a national company, how could you lose? You could compete with anyone.

Over the next twenty years I kept tweaking our operations until I felt we had a good comprehensive system. This system I developed would not only work for our business but would work for any business.

Goals of This Book

You have spent good money on this book because you are looking for a result. I'm not going to waste your time with a lot of fluff, or "how I did it" nonsense.

What I offer here is a simple step-by-step guide to build a business operating system in YOUR business - no matter what type of business you own.

It requires your buy-in and for you to implement the steps. But I assure you it isn't that difficult. Especially when you compare doing these steps to what it took you to build your business in the first place.

If you are just in the planning stages of your business, that's even better news. It is easier to start with an operating system in place rather than having to teach employees and managers a new system.

As a bonus to this system, I am adding one more important aspect to running a business that I believe most businesses are not aware of. I call it the Oyster, or the vibe of your business. This is something that costs nothing to implement but has a profound effect on how customers interact with your business. It will give you a huge leg up on your competition and I promise you, you will never look at another business in the same way.

SECTION 1:
The Bones

STEP 1:

Identify Your Hours of Operation

The typical way an entrepreneur will open a business is to first figure out all the things that need to be done. For example, for a simple retail store, someone needs to man the counter while the business is open. It makes sense that the entrepreneur will perform this job.

As for doing the daily deposits and going to the bank, the entrepreneur can do this before the store is open. So, if she opens at 10:00AM she has plenty of time to take care of any banking beforehand.

As for managing inventory, orders can be made while she is open during slow times of the day. Re-stocking can be performed after hours.

To be open more than five days per week, she could hire a high school student to cover on a weekend day. The entrepreneur will simply open and close for the employee. That should work.

This sounds like a simple system. However, you can already see some stress points in this plan. For one, because so much is dependent on the entrepreneur, the store hours are limited. In addition, this schedule will burn out the entrepreneur within a few years. What happens if there is a medical emergency, and the entrepreneur cannot go to work?

This example is just for a simple small retail shop. It gets more complicated for a restaurant, or a contractor, or a real estate office.

Let's back up to the retail store and approach it with a business operating system in mind.

A Retail Store

As an entrepreneur who plans on selling clothes, your goal is to have a great business. If you approach your business trying to make something that you would want to shop in, rather than the type of hours you want to work, it will change your whole paradigm on creating your business in the first place.

The top priority will be to establish operating hours that make sense to the customer and the business environment. It's possible that the store could be closed one day per week. This is a nice breather for the business and allows for any repair work to be done while the business is not open.

However, if the store is in an area where there is a lot of foot traffic seven days per week, then it would make sense that the business is open every day.

Most retail shops around the location do not open until 10AM, so this would be a good time to open as well. An entrepreneur would figure on an eight-hour day, but following a business system, you would set your hours to capture the most amount of business.

If in your area people are working during the day, it doesn't make sense to close your shop just as your customers are getting off work. Also, if the store was in a busy Downtown area, you might consider staying open later Friday and Saturday night when customers are in the area going to restaurants and theaters.

Based on customer needs and the location of your store, you decide to be open:

Monday through Thursday 10AM to 6PM

Friday and Saturday 10AM to 9PM

Sunday closed

Let's look at some other examples.

A Coffee House

Your research into the coffee business shows most of your customers are grabbing coffee to go from their vehicle on their way to work.

The main goal of your coffee house is to sell coffee and some light food items and not to be a restaurant, so in your research you get up very early in the morning and count cars going by your proposed location. This may sound old fashioned, but simply counting cars and observing the kind of traffic - tradesmen going to a job, or businesspeople in nice cars, or moms transporting children - can give you a lot more information about your customer base than what you can get using a Google search.

You notice that there is a mix of early traffic but mostly trades people in pickup trucks on their way to a job. Then at 6:30 AM the traffic picks up significantly with office workers heading their place of employment. By 9:00 AM the traffic dies down and you notice more SUVs with small children.

The traffic patterns stay relatively the same including the lunch hour. You see no spikes in the afternoon either.

On the weekends there is hardly any traffic until it starts to trickle in at 7:00AM and is really built up between 9:00AM and 10:00AM, then stays steady until about 2:00PM.

Your goal is to capture that early traffic, and to do that you know you want all hands-on deck to get coffee and maybe breakfast burritos available as efficiently and fast as you can.

Based on your observations you decide on business hours of seven days per week:

Monday through Friday 6:00AM to 2:00PM

Saturday and Sunday 7:00AM to 3:00PM

A Grocery Store

After traveling on vacation where you noticed a better quality of grocery store than you have in your town you get the itch to open one of your own that will specialize in more gourmet products that would appeal to customers who want healthier and better choices in their food buying.

Right off you can tell that you will be competing with a big box grocery store chain, so you must provide what they do not. Price will be a major concern and there is no way you will be able to compete on price.

You won't be able to have the hours they offer either, because you know it will cost so much to staff a small store equal to what a large store has.

To keep overhead to a minimal, you informally ask friends on Facebook and Instagram when they do their shopping during the week. You also start hanging out in the parking lot of the big box store to see when there is the most traffic and when the lax times are.

Right away you know you need to be open early and late on Saturday and Sunday. But you also need to be open during the week as well, because you need to be rotating through the fresh produce.

Since you will have a deli in your store you need to be open for lunch too. After careful research and discussion with your spouse you make your decision on hours.

Monday through Friday 10:00AM to 8:00PM

Saturday and Sunday 10:00AM to 8:00PM

A Real Estate Office

Having worked for other real estate offices, and having a broker's license, you decide to strike out on your own. Why should you split your commission with the owner-broker when you are the one doing all the work?

Your past office was in a strip mall, and it was just a place where contracts could be written up and a hub where real estate agents could work out of.

You want to be in a place where you could attract some attention from people passing by, so you need a location that has foot traffic.

However, it also needs to have adequate parking as well for people to have easy access for appointments. One other thing that matters to you is that the office be aesthetically appealing.

When the office is open to the public isn't as great a need as most of the communication with potential customers is through social media. However, a location with foot traffic is going to be most busy on weekends so that is when you want to have the office occupied and presented in some sort of way that will attract customers through the door.

Other than that, a posted sign on the door and through social media with a contact number for messaging and a guarantee of a return call within 2 minutes should satisfy most others.

In this new office you choose very simple hours, at least to start. With more business you will be able to hire someone to be in the office more.

Monday through Friday by appointment

Saturday and Sunday 10:00AM to 6:00PM

80/20 And Your Hours

As a new business with limited resources, you want to catch as much business as possible with the least amount of overhead. Most of that overhead will be in the form of labor, so the less the better.

I will add a very large caveat to this, however. You may decide to bite the bullet and start with expanded hours so your potential customers can count on you to be open. The LAST thing you want to do is post hours that state Open 7 days per week from 10:00AM until?

I've seen this posted, especially in restaurants, and the owner might as well put out a sign that say "Hey, we are amateurs here!" If a customer drives to your place and expects you to be open and you are not, you can bet they won't make that mistake again.

We had an Italian Restaurant we opened on old Route 66 in Albuquerque, and we wanted to be open late, as there were no other places where someone could get a late meal except for Denny's. We posted our hours as 4:00PM to 11:00PM. I swear no one came in that first year after 10:00PM but we still had staff on just in case they did. We came close to pulling the plug on that idea but held firm to the commitment. After that first-year people started trickling in late after a movie let out, or they had been at the bars or dancing. By the end of the second year, we had a really good late-night business.

However, if you need to start as simple as possible, do your research and use the 80/20 principle for your hours. The 80/20 principle means 80% of your profits come from 20% of your efforts.

For example, if you were a coffee house open from 6:00AM until 4:00PM and you looked at your sales by hour. You probably would find that 80% of your sales occurred between 7:00AM and 11:00AM. The 20% is probably from 11:00AM until 4:00PM with a little bump at noon.

If I had limited money to spend on labor, I might start out selling coffee just from 7:00 until 11:00. As business grew, I would expand my hours as I could afford more help and there was customer demand. It looks better to the customer to see you expand your hours rather than take them away. So, start small.

Step 1
Action Item

- Research your location to see when the optimum hours of operation would be for your business

- Narrow those hours down to where you believe the 80% of your business will come from.

STEP 2:

Identify Positions

An entrepreneur opening a business will look at the personalities involved to make the business operate, then decide who is best suited for what kind of work. This is not the way to go about it.

Your first priorities are to identify what the jobs are to be done, or more specifically what are the roles employees will engage in to properly operate your business.

You see it doesn't matter the person's name in that role, but the role itself. You can fill in the names later for each role. In fact, at the beginning it may be the same person filling many different roles. But as you grow, that one person can step out of a role to be replaced by a new employee and this doesn't affect the business in the least.

No matter what type of business you plan to open, after you have figured out what the best hours of operation are, you must now decide what are the positions in your organization that need to be filled.

You don't think of your business as a little mom and pop shop, but rather the first of 3,000. It's as if you plan on opening a national chain of businesses. To do a good job, you need to remove the personalities and instead focus on the individual positions that will make your business run smoothly.

Let's go back to our examples and fill in the possible positions as an illustration.

The Retail Store

There are obvious jobs that need to be done in a typical retail store.

Obviously, you need a **Salesclerk** to stand behind the counter and ring up the transactions for your customers and answer any questions that they may have.

You also need a **General Manager**. This is the person who oversees the whole shop. The ultimate responsibility for this store rests on this person's shoulders.

A **Shift Manager** would be a good addition also. Given the hours of operation, you can't have the General Manager working 7-days per week. There needs to be someone with responsibility to get the doors open and closed who is there on the days the General Manager is not. It is possible that the Shift Manager as well as the General Manager while working also work as a Salesclerk.

There should also be a **bookkeeper** to do the daily books and make the deposits. This person will not only go to the bank but also input sales information into an accounting software like QuickBooks, and to be able to do the bank reconciliations at the end of the month.

They would also handle all accounts payable and receivable, as well as payroll, if that is done in-house.

Again, the General Manager my perform some of these duties and even the Shift Manager could go to the bank on the days the General Manager is off.

There could be other positions depending on the type of retail store you plan. This may include:

- **Delivery Person**
- **Stocker**
- **Web and Marketing Person**
- **Personnel Manager**

A Coffee House

I have some experience with this one. We used to own a coffee house in Santa Fe, New Mexico, which evolved from a small kiosk selling coffee, to a full-blown coffee house cafe.

Back then I didn't follow this plan and didn't even know about it. The kiosk was separate from our large Italian restaurant, so all we did was have an extra employee out there to sell cups of coffee. But as in most cases with business, it grew.

If I were opening a coffee house today, I would start by outlining the positions in the coffee house. These would include:

- **Barista** someone to make the coffee
- **Shift Manager** someone in charge for the day
- **General Manager** this person has the main responsibility for the operations of the coffee house

- **Cook** this person, if food is to be served, even if it is just muffins and scones would prepare the items.

- **Bookkeeper** to do the daily books, payroll, accounts payable and receivables

- **Maintenance Person** who oversees the repairs necessary to keep the equipment functioning and the facility in good repair.

A Grocery Store

Like any business there has to be someone in charge and someone who does the work. In a Grocery store there are many jobs, even if it is just you and another. While you will perform many of the jobs yourself, you still of course need to list what those jobs would be.

- **Cashier** to check people out

- **Bagger** to bag groceries for customers or the customers do it themselves

- **Stocker** which is a constant thing in the grocery business

- **Shift Manager** who could also be a Cashier or Stocker, but is responsible also for opening or closing, getting change and trouble shooting

- **Bookkeeper to do the daily books, payroll, accounts payable and accounts receivable**

- **General Manager** to oversee the entire operation

- **Deli Manager** in charge of prepared foods

- **Deli Cook** to prepare foods to go

- **Janitor** to clean the store.

A Real Estate Office

Assuming your business will grow, there is more than one position that needs to be filled in this office. You are the owner and have a broker's license, which could also be considered the general manager since you are the one where the buck stops. For a fully functioning office set-up you might consider these positions.

- **Owner/Broker** Basically the general manager

- **Associate Agent** The real estate agents you hire

- **Receptionist Someone** to answer the phones, but could also be filled by Associate Agents on a rotating basis

- **Administrative Assistant** This person coordinates the paperwork for each deal and helps with closings

When you come up with positions in your business you are not thinking of who will fill those positions. Remember you are creating a business as though it is the first one of 3,000. The template for your business can simply be taken to the next town in your expansion. From there you will hire people into those positions.

Even if you never open another location, going through this exercise sets your business to run **whether you are there or not**. This is the key to a successful business. You want to create a business that does not depend on the owner actually being in the business. In other words, this is one step closer to making a system where you work on your business and not in your business. I will repeat this important fact many times in this book. Remember, you don't go into Starbucks expecting to see the owner.

Step 2
Action Items

· Identify the positions in your business

· Exclude names of individuals, and rather just list the actual titles of each position

STEP 3:
Training Checklists
For Each Position

Somewhere in your background, probably in high school, you worked in a place where the way you were trained you spent a couple of days following around a more experienced worker who showed you the ropes. After that you were on your own.

You made plenty of mistakes but over time you learned your job, and even helped train others who came along after you.

The problem with this system is it's similar to the game of **Telephone.** An employee learns from the boss to do the job the way the boss wants it done. Over time the employee invents shortcuts and new methods, which they pass on to the employee they train. That employee also figured out some shortcuts, which they pass along, and so on. Then about a year later the owner sees an employee doing something that is completely wrong and asks the employee why? The employee says, "that's the way it's always been done."

There is another aspect to this system as well. I learned it when I was a young manager, which I mentioned in the introduction to this book, called **Management by Abdication.**

It's tempting to just make a problem go away. So, you hire an employee who seems like they would be good at a job you need done and they can take care of it. I see this all the time. The owner doesn't really want to work in the business and especially doesn't want to work *on* the business. Instead, the owner hires a professional who has experience in that area and sets them loose.

There is a better way, and the only way a professional business operates. It is through rigorous training. In this section we want to create a system for training these employees, so that it is consistent going forward in your business.

As the business progresses, the content will change as the business changes, but the system of training will stay the same, or be improved upon but under a plan and not shooting from the hip.

The Perfect Employee

I have found that the best way for me to make up a training checklist for a position in my business, is to first think about what the perfect employee would be in that job.

For example, if I was creating a training checklist for a bartender in my brewpub, the perfect bartender would have a good personality, could move fast, would know how to pour a pint of beer with a one-inch head on it, would understand how to recognize if someone had too much to drink and how to tactfully cut someone off. They would understand how beer is made and be able to explain it to a customer. Of course, they would have to know how to wash glasses, work the point-of-sale system, prioritize their tasks, and know how to upsell when taking orders - "Would you like a 16 oz. pint or an English 20-ounce pint?".

Then there is the laundry list of things they need to know as well, like where to park, how to make a schedule request, what the paydays are, what to wear, what employee discounts are available along with a whole host of small details that make up the job. These types of training items are repeated for all positions.

If you were training a salesclerk in your clothing store, the perfect salesclerk would acknowledge each guest as they walked into the door. They would be able to make recommendations and be able to listen to the customer and discern what the customer really wants. They would have no problem dealing with customer returns, but also making suggestions of items that might go along with what the customer is purchasing, thereby upselling.

As I mentioned previously, each training checklist will contain some basic information that every employee must know. This could include:

Pay schedule

Time off requests

Where to park

When breaks are taken

Uniform and appearance

Disciplinary actions

Hours of operation

Employee benefits

The list will be the same for each position and something that every employee needs to know.

After these items, you list the things that you want that perfect employee to know. Each of these items are specific to that position. You don't need to get too complicated at this point. Just make the list as inclusive as you can for what little you know yourself, as this is a new business, and you still aren't sure how it will all shake out.

As time goes on you will amend this training checklist to include new items and discard the old ones.

This is the foundation of the whole business system. You need to have a well-trained staff and that staff needs to be trained consistently from one employee to another. This is especially true if you have any sort of employee turn-over.

Don't sweat it too much. You can edit it down later, just get some information on a piece of paper. You could create these if you put your mind to it in one hour. Just get it done.

If you have made a list of the positions in your business, your next step is to create a training checklist for each position. Even if you know that it is you who will be doing most of the positions in your new business, you still need to go through this exercise and establish these training sheets.

It won't be too long until you need to hire someone, as you can't do it all yourself for long, and when you do, you need to train that person in the position you hired for.

Step 3
Action Items

- Make a list of the qualities for the perfect employee for each position

- Included on your training checklist of those qualities you have identified, also include the basics that every position will need, like where to park, what to wear, etc.

STEP 4:
Daily Checklists

One day, quite a while ago as my partners and I were just starting our first restaurant, I was traveling somewhere and was waiting for a connecting flight at the airport. Sitting at a gate by the window, I could see our plane being cleaned for the next flight. I noticed the pilot walking around the plane with a clipboard in his hand. The pilot - I knew he was because of the four stripes on the shoulder boards on his uniform - seemed to be checking things off on the clipboard. I thought at the time this must be some sort of pre-flight checklist. I doubt they do that anymore, at least the walking around part outside of the airplane, but currently I believe that is what they were doing. I asked some people at the counter, and they confirmed it for me.

The pilot had just the right amount of grey hair, which indicated to me that he had plenty of flying experience, yet I could see, even with what I imagined were thousands of hours in the air, he still was using a simple check list on a clipboard to check everything before we took off.

I thought to myself, "If this person is using a checklist to make sure everything is done correctly, then surely our employees should have a checklist as well".

Without a checklist you are relying on your memory. This pilot had probably flown thousands of times and I'm sure could go through the checklist by memory, yet there he was with the physical checklist in his hands.

The purpose of the checklist is to remind the person who is in that job to make sure all the items are checked off. It's that simple yet can get abandoned once the employee knows his or her job so well, that they think they don't need the checklist anymore. This is a mistake.

Even if an employee comes into work and goes through all the things that are on the checklist by memory, they should still go back and consult the checklist to see if they forgot anything.

This way all the items that need to be done on the checklist are actually done consistently, every day. A checklist is not set in stone either. It can be changed depending on how the job evolves, or the time of year, the hours of operation based on seasonality, or anything else that changes during normal business maturity.

Let's look at some examples.

Retail Store Clerk

Opening

- Clock in
- Sweep Counter Area

- Restock Supplies
- Straighten Shelves

Closing

- Restock Merchandise
- Do Sales Reports
- Clean Counter
- Check Fitting Rooms
- Take Trash out
- Clock Out

The list can be much longer of course based on the type of retail store and everything that you would want to include in the opening and closing sections.

Coffee House Barista

Opening

- Clock In
- Stock Coffee Supplies
- Count Cash Register ($150)
- Check refrigeration Temperatures
- Sweep & Mop Floors
- Set Music and Lights

Closing

- Put Chairs on Tables and Sweep
- Take Trash out
- Ring out Cash Register
- Wipe Down Sinks
- Clean Out Refrigerators
- Have Manager Check Out
- Clock Out

A Grocery Store Register Person

Opening

- Clock In
- Count Drawer
- Check Todays Sales Promotions
- Stock Check Out Supplies
- Clean Check Out Area

Closing

- Restock Check Out Supplies
- Pull Cash Drawer and ring out Cash Register
- Check Out with Manager
- Clock Out

Real Estate Office

Opening

- Vacuum & Polish Furniture
- Set Lights and Music
- Arrange Fresh Flowers
- Update Current Listings
- Put Sandwich Board Sign Out on Sidewalk
- Make Coffee and Set Up Candy Bowl for Customers

Closing

- Pull in Sandwich Board
- Clean Coffee Station
- Empty Trash
- Send out Follow Up Emails to Customers
- Turn Off Lights and Music

These lists would be much longer based on your own knowledge of what you want each position to do. I have just given examples, but in my experience in restaurants, our positions had checklists that were a full page at least.

I typically would also include an item on the checklist that has the manager on duty check out the employee to see that they did everything on their lists.

In my experience, many employees will simply check off most of the items on their list without doing the jobs. You will find when the next shift takes over an employee complains that the work wasn't done from the previous shift. That's why you should have a manager check out each employee. Every employee, every shift.

Again, when you make up the daily checklist for each position, it doesn't have to be perfect right from the start. As the weeks go by you will be adding things and subtracting others that are no longer needed. It is as simple as going onto your computer where you have these checklists and editing them to your current needs. Then print it up, laminate it, and replace the old one on the clipboard with the new copy. Heck, to start with you could just handwrite one on a yellow legal pad.

The key here is to get your organization used to the checklists as a normal part of their job. Don't worry about making it pretty, just make it available.

Step 4
Action Items

- Create a daily checklist for each position.

- On each checklist, divide it between opening and closing procedures it appropriate

STEP 5:
Side-work

Every business looks great when you first open the doors, however given time things just start to fall apart. One of the reasons to have an operating system is to maintaining consistency in your business, and that includes keeping the place looking well kept.

Some businesses hire outside services to maintain their facility, and of course that is important with maintenance items that are too complicated to be done in-house.

However, you also have in your business employees who can perform small jobs that will keep the business looking sharp. The key is to spread all the small jobs out over your list of employees. If each employee does just one thing extra each day, it will have a huge impact on the physical plant of your business.

That's why I like to include a section in the middle of the daily employee checklist of side-work to be performed.

All of this depends on the of business you are in and the type of facility you occupy. For example, if the business has a lot of customers walking in and out of the door, like a restaurant, bar, grocery store or coffeehouse, the place will wear out much faster than a clothing store, lawyers office or real estate office.

However even in an office there are plenty of small jobs that can be performed each day that will really make a difference in the overall look of your business.

It helps to walk through your business and specifically the areas where each position works. When you are looking at that area, make a note of things that need attention above and beyond what typically that employee would do every day.

This can be really simple things that maybe you haven't thought of. For example, in an office are the lamps dusted. And speaking of dusted, whenever I am in a business and use the restroom, I look up at the vent above the toilet. If it looks like it is growing a beard because of all the accumulated dust, I know there is no system managing this business. So maybe once a week, an employee goes into the restroom with a wet rag and dusts that vent. It takes about two minutes for one employee but will keep it looking like someone cares.

Another gripe I have in restaurants, bars and coffee houses are the floor sinks behind the bar. These are typically white porcelain sinks flush with the floor that everything drains into. The porcelain gets stained over time and can look pretty disgusting. The truth is your customers can't see this, but that's beside the point. Remember, you want to own a well-run business, so even this sink needs to stay clean.

This can be simply achieved on an employee's daily checklist with the use a little cleanser and then scrub it out once or twice a week. So,

I would add it as side-work to the Tuesday and Saturday sheets. This will keep it white and clean.

Now that you have already made a checklist for each position that includes opening and closing procedures, you next insert into the middle of that checklist a side-work section.

Let's say you have a gift shop on a main street in a historic downtown. The main position for this shop is the salesclerk and you have created an opening checklist as well as a closing checklist since there is only one employee when you are open.

In between the opening checklist and the closing checklist you would insert your side-work checklist and it would look something like this.

Salesclerk

Opening

- Adjust air-conditioner/heat
- Sweep
- Restock Supplies
- Clean Restroom, check paper goods
- Count Cash Drawer
- Straighten Shelves
- Turn on music
- Adjust lights
- Sweep Sidewalk
- Windex Glass Counter-top

- Put out Sandwich Board on sidewalk
- Turn on open sign and unlock door
- Check GM Book

Side-Work

- Monday - Dust lights
- Tuesday - Change Sales Display
- Wednesday - Touch up paint if needed
- Thursday - Polish Wood
- Friday - Deep Clean of Restroom
- Saturday - Clean Glass Door
- Sunday - Come up with one sales promotion idea

Closing

- Bring in Sandwich Board
- Lock door and make sure no one is in store
- Turn off open sign
- Ring out Register
- Count money and place in drop box safe
- Take trash out
- Reorganize shelves
- Turn off lights and music
- Make sure door is locked when you leave

There would be similar daily checklists for each position in any sort of business you can think of. As you can see, there are so many tiny details to operating a business that may seem small, but put together, really can make a difference.

Once you have this format in your computer, it is a simple operation to make small changes as you need to. For example, in the summer you may need to add an item about watering the flowers. Or, if you are so busy you add a second clerk, you may need to divide the lists up and think of more things you would like to have done.

The possibilities just keep expanding as you become more familiar with operating your business.

Step 5
Action Items

· Add a side-work section into the middle of your daily checklists

· Add at least one extra thing that needs to be done on each day that you are open

STEP 6:

The GM Book

So far you have done a pretty good job at organizing the details needed to operate your business, but wait! There's more!

We have identified what positions are in our business so that it runs based on positions rather than individual personalities (which can and will change). We next created training checklists for each of those positions so that the staff is trained to cover all the things you as the owner feel are important, and they are trained consistently as time goes by.

Next, we created a simple checklist for each position so that when an employee comes to work, they have a framework to operate under, which will make sure all the small important things are done to open and close for business each day.

Into this we have added a section for side-work, which will keep your business looking well-cared for.

But what about the things that need to be done just every so often?

We can't leave it up to our memory alone to perform these tasks, and they don't need to be done on a weekly basis, so these things won't go on the daily checklist.

To get the "every-so-often" things done, we create a **GM Book**. GM stands for General Maintenance but can include really anything you need to be reminded to do.

To make a GM Book, get a simple three-ring binder. Next go to an office supply and get dividers for this book that are made for a calendar month. There would be 31 of these dividers. They are made for this and sold in most office supply stores. Put these in your binder and add a simple sheet of paper in between each one. That's basically it.

Now you need to fill it out. To do that, start thinking of things you need to do every so often. The GM Book will be your reminder.

For example, if you have a restaurant, you might add

CLEAN OUT COMPRESSOR SCREENS ON REACH IN COOLERS

Maybe add this on day 5 and day 18. Refrigeration fails usually from dirty compressor screens so that the compressor can't cool sufficiently. Changing a compressor is very expensive, so taking a damp cloth and wiping the accumulated dust off these screens will help insure a longer life for your refrigeration unit.

Let's say you are in a city and the visitors Bureau puts out a list of upcoming events on the 12th of each month. I would add on the sheet in the divider marker 12

CHECK VISITORS BUREAU WEB SITE FOR UPCOMING EVENTS

Knowing if there is a convention of Astrophysicists coming to town, you might want to do a special promotion for that group to get them into your store.

You may need a reminder when certain taxes need to be paid, and you would add that to the GM Book as well.

You might want to do employee evaluations on a certain day, and this in your book will be an excellent reminder.

The layout of a retail store can get boring, so why not pick a day during the month to move displays around so that returning customers feel like they are seeing something new?

One thing you will want to do however, is to add onto your daily checklist to check and do what is in the GM book for that day. The managers daily checklist should therefore have, Check GM Book as one of the checklist items.

If for example you are in February and there is something posted on the 29th, 30th, or 31st, then on the 28th you should also look on the next days and do those items as well just so you make sure everything is completed. You could also try not to schedule extra things on those last three pages.

The GM Book is one of the most useful tools in this whole system. It acts as a catch-all for all the crumbs of small to-do's you need to accomplish each month that aren't on your daily employee checklists.

When you build it, don't sweat the details. The book will write itself. You can add a few things to get you started, but as the year progresses, you will find other things that you need to remember going forward and you can add those to your GM Book.

Step 6
Action Items

- Purchase three-ring binder

- Add 31 dividers to represent one month. Place a piece of paper after each number

- Add items you want to remember on certain days of the month that have to do with your business

STEP 7:
The Internal Audit

So far, we've come up with a pretty good business system that takes care of all the details that need to be performed to operate your business. Of course, operating a business is so much more than just a bunch of checklists, but the checklists give your business a framework in which to operate.

Now, do you think your employees, or even your managers are going to follow this system? No, they won't.

A typical scenario in a business that has many employees would be like this.

The employee comes to work and grabs her checklist but doesn't need to check it because she has been on the job for months and has it memorized.

At the end of her shift, she tells the manager that she is done. The manager, who is counting the cash drawer, asks if she did her side-work and she says yes.

The next day a different employee comes in and sees the work that wasn't done and complains to the manager. By then though it is too late, and the scenario starts all over again.

With the internal audit, the managers will check to see that the systems that have been set up are followed.

To make an internal audit sheet, I like to divide the business up into sections. For example, in a restaurant, I might have an audit sheet for the bar area, for the dining room, for the kitchen, and maybe even a separate one for the restrooms. This would be done for any business. Just divide up the office or retail space into sections.

On an audit sheet you want to list whatever you are looking at in that area that might need attention. The walls, floor and ceiling, the lights all clean and working, the wood polished, the vents all clean from dust, the sidewalk clean and free of cigarette butts.

If there is only one general manager and one shift manager, then I would divide the audit sheet into two section and divide it how you see fit.

The idea is that at any time during the week you, the auditor in charge of your section, will walk through and look at all the things on the list and make sure they are all in order.

If your employees are doing their checklists, then your audit will be fine. If, however they are not, maybe because a manager didn't check them out when they left, then something will show up on your audit sheet. It is now up to you, the person doing the audit, to correct the problem yourself, but also to find out what happened that the employee didn't do their side-work. You want to make sure it doesn't happen again, so you make sure the checklist system is being used correctly so that everything gets done.

All these internal audit sheets are saved on a clipboard, as proof that the internal audit has been completed. I'll explain in the next step why.

However, with an internal audit, the managers have a system to make sure the basic function of the regular checklists are being followed, thereby keeping your business looking sharp.

In addition to the physical things that need to be cleaned and in good repair, I also include some financial goals as well, that I will explain a little bit later.

These financial goals that must be met will be on all internal audit sheets, as all the managers play a role in meeting these targets.

If you are a one-person operation, fulfilling many roles your internal audit sheet will simply cover your entire business. It's tempting to just let this go as you are by yourself, but please don't. You won't always be alone and if you are doing a good job and following the system, your business will grow. If you aren't doing all the steps at this point, you won't suddenly change and start doing them later.

These are just good habits to form at the beginning of your business adventure. Any one of them take only a few minutes but provide mountains of solid business success. Remember successful businesses don't just happen. To stay in business over the long-haul, they need the tools to carry them through the years.

We are almost done with checklists, but not quite yet.

Step 7
Action Items

· Divide your business into physical sections

· List everything in each section you want to examine to make sure that all the checklists are being followed

· Perform a weekly Internal Audit of these sections once per week

STEP 8:
The External Audit

As I mentioned earlier, all these checklists and internal audit sheets really do cover all the physical aspects of your business, but now do you think your employees, or your managers are really going to follow them? Again, probably not.

It's time to put some teeth into the system. We will do this by creating an external audit sheet.

This sheet is like the internal audit; however, it combines everything on those audits into one sheet.

The external audit is performed once per month and can happen at any time, but it is important that it be random.

Also, the external audit should not (in most cases) be performed by you the owner. Find a friend, or associate, or family member to do this important task. You should pay them for this service as well, either with a paycheck, or maybe even a trade for goods or services.

To make an external audit sheet, combine the areas of the business onto the page (s) but also add a point value to each item. You've heard of the business adage that "You can't manage it without quantifying it." By assigning points to each audit item, you will be giving a score to the audit sheet, which in turn, quantifies your business system.

To make the point system simple, I like to make everything add up to 100. We are used to scores that have a high point of 100, so if we see a score of 92, we instinctively know that's good, and one of 65, not so much. This will make an audit score more real than just a simple sheet with no score at all.

Here is a sample audit sheet from one of my brewpubs.

Kitchen

1	Floors Clean - under equipment as well as center
1	Walls Clean - entire prerimeter
1	Sinks Clean
1	Hand Sink - Sotcked w/ paper towels and hand soap
1	Oven Clean - inside and outside
1	Lights - working and dusted
1	Reach Ins Clean - inside, around inserts & Compressor
1	Shellves Clean and organised
1	Table & Countertops clean
1	Food Temps 40 degrees or below
1	Thermometers in Coolers
1	Pass Through Clean
1	Drain & Screen Clean
1	Dough Mixer Clean
1	Microwave Clean
1	Hood Clean & Screen
1	Dish Machine Clean

Brewery

1	Wall Paint Clean & No Chips
1	Cove Base Clean
1	Floors Clean No Mold
1	Tanks Polished
1	Floor Drain Clean
1	Sink Clean
1	Window Sills Clean & Organized
1	Walk In Floor Clean
1	Ceiling Fan & Light Clean
1	Grain Storage Area Clean & Organized

Restroom

1	Sink Clean Including Faucets
1	Toilet Clean Including Base
1	Floors Clean
1	Vent Clean
1	Paper & Soap Stocked With Back Ups Available
1	Walls Clean & In Good Repair
1	Mirror Clean
1	Lights Working & Dusted
1	Door Clean Including Handle And Frame
1	Vanity & Merchandis Clean
1	Window Sill Clean

Outside

1	Table Surface Clean
1	Grounds Swept Free Of Trash
1	Window Sills Clean
1	Bricks Free Of Cobwebs
1	Ash Tray Clean

AUDIT SCORE_____

DATE_____

Bar

1	3 Comp. Sink Clean
1	Hand Sink Clean with Soap Available
1	Both Floor Drains Clean
1	Floor Clean (under sinks, behind coolers,)
1	Brass Clean (Taps, Beer Engine, Rail)
1	Front of bar Clean
1	Wood Work on Back Bar Clean & Dust Free
1	Lights Working & Dust Free
1	Register Areas Neat And Organized. (both plus drawer)
1	Bottles and Shelf Clean and Dust Free
1	Matting Clean
1	Silverware Table Clean & Organized
1	Shelf Under Pizza Window Clean
1	Beer Menu Lights Work and Dust Free
1	Divider From Bar and Brewery Clean and Organized

Dining Room

1	Wall Paint Clean & No Chips
1	Cove Base Clean
1	Table Bases Clean
1	Window Sills Clean
1	Lights in Window Sills Dusted & Working
1	Fans Dusted
1	Clock, Painting, Mirrors Clean
1	Table Tops Clean
1	Front Door In Good Repair
1	Merchandise Shelves Clean & Stocked (tees, oil, books)
1	Chairs & Stools Clean
1	Upholstery Benches Clean & In Good Repair
1	Front Of Bar Clean
1	Floors Clean & In Good Repair

Laundry Area & Office

1	Floor Clean Laundry Room
1	Washer/Dryer Clean - Inside and Out
1	Shelves Clean and Organised
1	Walls Clean
1	Kitchen Hallway Wall Clean & Good Repair
1	Stairs Swept
1	Base of Stairs Clean & Organized
1	Office Floor Vaccuumed & Swept
1	Desk Top & Drawers Organized
1	Merchandise Organized & Neat
1	Office Supplies Organized & Neat
1	Lights Working
1	No Cobwebs
1	Vaccuum Cleaner Emptied

Business

2	Score Board Up To Date
3	All COGS in Black
3	Labor Budget in Black
2	Change Bank Counted
2	Bills Coded and Filed
2	Deposits Match DSR

The external audit brings a fresh pair of eyes onto your operation, which in turn keeps you honest. Most national companies have some sort of system similar to this. Most small businesses do not.

With this last checklist, you tie a nice ribbon onto your business system, but there is one more thing that pulls the whole thing together.

Step 9

Action Items

- Combine all your internal audit sheet sections into one all-encompassing sheet we will call an external audit.

- Assign points to each item that can add up to 100

- Find someone outside your organization who will do this audit once a month, unannounced and at any time.

STEP 9:
The Manager Meeting

So far, so good. You have:

- Identified the positions in your business

- Made a training checklist for each position

- Made a daily checklist for each position

- Added a side-work duty to each daily checklist

- Captured all the other things that need to be done every so often in a GM Book

- Created an internal audit so managers can make sure the area of the business they oversee is following your system

- Made an external audit sheet so that the managers are using the system

Now comes a way to pull everything together to keep your business growing.

The way I see it is the system we have put together is like a skeleton. It forms the basic functions that keep the business looking good with some consistency. This system will work for practically any business, so just like how we humans are all so different and yet have the same skeletal structure, so too could you have a bike shop and also a separate clothing store and they would have the same business system, only the checklists would be different.

It's one thing to have that basic system in place, but another to stay fresh and be able to change fast when the economy changes, the market changes, the seasons change, etc. To do this you need to have good communication with the principals in your business to make the timely decisions that are needed.

A weekly manager meeting can accomplish this. Don't roll your eyes, meetings are still important, and having one every week will keep all the managers on the same page and can address problems before they become too big.

Keep the meetings short if you can and make an agenda to follow. There is nothing worse than a long-drawn-out meeting where one person dominates and drones on and on.

Topics to go over include:

- Going over the audit sheets
- Employees good and bad
- Financials
- Upcoming events
- Open discussion

Keep the meeting under an hour and try to meet at the same time every week so everyone involved can plan their weeks around it. Also, if the managers are on hourly wage, then they should clock in and get paid for the meeting.

This is a simple step, but really the manager meeting caps the whole checklist system you have made for your business.

In the next section we will go through some additional things that you can incorporate into your business system. There are some great things to add, but even if you didn't add anything more to your business system than what these 10 steps covered, you are 99% better than your competition that just goes to work and deals with issues as they come up with no system at all. Please do the steps.

Step 9
Action Items

- Pick a time once per week to meet with your key people

- Keep the meeting under one hour!

SECTION 2:
The Muscle

STEP 10:
The Scoreboard

When you look at a Profit and Loss (P&L) statement, you can think of the way it is laid out as your to-do list. It's already prioritized for you.

The first line on your P&L is Sales. Think about it, what could be more important that sales? Without sales there is no business. Sales provide the cash to operate your business, pay for the goods you sell, pay yourself and your employees and all the other expenses associated with your business. Everything you do contributes to your sales to keep them strong and growing. So naturally this is your fist priority.

Typically, the second item on any retail establishment P&L will be your Cost of Sales. This refers to the wholesale items you need to buy and then sell to your customers. This can be in raw form that you put together to sell as in widgets in a factory or food ingredients in a bakery, or items ready to sell like clothes in a clothing store.

It's the second biggest thing because in most cases it is your largest expense. What you pay for your wholesale goods will reflect directly to what is left over at the bottom of your P&L in the form of net profit.

The third largest item, and it may be your second largest item, is Labor. Not only labor, but labor taxes as well. For every $1 you spend in labor you also contribute up to 20 cents in associated labor taxes. A dollar saved here goes right to your bottom line, so efficiency and productivity is incredibly important.

These three things are what we want to concentrate on. Why? Because of Vilfredo Pareto.

Thank You Vilfredo Pareto

Vilfredo Pareto (1848-1923) was an Italian philosopher, engineer, sociologist, and economist. He was well known for his study of income distribution. Particularly he noticed that 80% of the land in Italy was owned by just 20% of the population. He also noticed that 80% of his peas came from just 20% of the peas he planted.

Basically, he was suggesting that 80% of your results can come from just 20% of your efforts. This has been born out repeatedly resulting in the name Pareto Principal.

You may find that 80% of your sales are coming from just 20% of the products you have for sale. Or it could be that 80% of your sales are coming from just 20% of your sales staff. Again and again, the Pareto Principal plays out in your business.

We want to use this principal to our advantage to save time and resources. This is where the scoreboard comes in.

Just a side note, if the only thing you get out of this book is that you start using a scoreboard, then it was well worth the price of admission.

When I opened my first business, I would go through the day-to-day operations, making deposits, doing my inventories, and working a lot of hours.

At the end of the month, I would give all my checking account ledgers and inventory totals to my accountant, who also did my payroll. This was usually by the 5th of the month.

Close to the middle of the month he would produce a profit and loss statement and then my partners and I would meet with him to go over this P&L to see how we did.

After about a year (I'm a little slow) I realized the information provided by the P&L wasn't really doing me any good. By the time we were analyzing the profit and loss statement, that month was long gone, and in fact the current month was half over as well.

I thought, wouldn't it make more sense to make the P&L you wanted, then work each day to make that happen in real time? To do this, we would have to create a budget.

We knew about what we thought our sales would be because we had been open for a year by then. We also knew what our cost of sales were going to be as we did monthly inventories and calculated it. Most of the monthly costs could be figured out as well, like rent, utilities, repairs, advertising, credit card fees and the like. The one wild card was labor. We would create a schedule for the month and calculate that out by multiplying the hours by the wages of the crew. That would give us our over-all labor estimate for the month.

With this number we could plug it into our budget and see if there was any money left over. If there wasn't, we could go back and try to cut labor a bit, or scale back on advertising or a few of the other small expenses so if we hit the projected sales volume, we knew we would make a profit.

This would be our starting point for the month. We were creating the P&L that we wanted to have, rather than waiting until the middle of the next month to see if we hit those numbers.

The key now was to work the business every day and keep an eye on the largest contributors of profitability. As I mentioned, using the Pareto Principal, we determined that sales, cost of sales, and labor was where we needed to concentrate on.

Build Your Scoreboard

We decided to make the tracking of these key numbers as simple as possible. After all, we had a business to run and couldn't afford to spend all our time in the office crunching numbers.

The first thing we did was to go out and buy a basic dry-erase board and two dry erase markers: one black and one red.

At the top of our scoreboard, we had a place to write the month, and how many days we would be open. Typically, we were open 7 days a week so it would say 31 or so.

SALES

Next, we would write *SALES BUDGET*, and next to this we would fill in what we hoped our sales objective would be.

Under this we next wrote *SALES PACE*. This is where would write a new number every day based on our sales to date and calculating our pace.

Pay Attention, this is important.

To calculate a Sales Pace. Let's say you are open 31 days. On day one your sales are $1,236. Since that is your first day, that is your average. You take the **average** sales to date and multiply it by how many days you will be open, in this case 31. $1,236 x 31 = $38,316. That is your sales pace as of day one.

The next day your sales are $1,352. To calculate your pace now you take the sales to date ($1,236 + $1,352 = $2,588) and divide by how many days you have been open so far. That is 2 days. So, $2,588 divided by 2 = $1,294. This is your new average. This gets multiplied by how many days you are open (31), and your new sales pace is $40,114.

If your budget for the month was $40,000 and as of day 2 your pace was $40,114, that means you are ahead of your sales projection. So, in the space next to Sales Pace, you would write $40,114. Because this is in positive territory you write this number in black. If the number was less than $40,000, like after your first day when it was $38,316, you would write that in red, because you are not meeting your budget. Red is bad. Black is good.

The first half of the month the pace swings around quite a bit as weekends may be better than the beginning of the week, and if you started the month on a Tuesday, you probably won't be hitting your pace until the weekend. Or, if you started the month out on a Friday, you would show a huge pace compared to your budget.

By the middle of the month the averages calm down and you can get a real sense of where your sales are heading. If they are staying strong and you are consistently hitting your budget goal, no worries.

But if by the middle of the month your sales pace is written in red every day, then you need to do something. You start coming up with sales promotions, specials, more advertising, whatever you can think of to increase sales to hit that budget number.

If this math seems cumbersome, then putting your daily sales into a Daily Sales Register (DSR) that is an Excel spreadsheet, which can calculate this for you. You can reach out to me, and I will send you an example spreadsheet you can use to do this.

See how you are creating your P&L in real time? Remember, sales are your number one priority, so this step is vital to the monthly success of your business.

Cost of Sales

The next section on your scoreboard is your Cost of Sales. This is how much you pay for the things you sell as a percentage of sales.

For example, if I sell a bottle of Mexican Coke, which costs .43 cents, and I sell it for $2.75, the percentage of sales is calculated by taking the .43 and dividing it by the sales price of $2.75. This comes out to 15.6%. If your goal for beverages was 20% then you are doing great with 15.6%.

That's fine for one item, but any retail establishment has many items they sell. Also, you must account for inventory you start the month out with, the inventory you purchase during the month, and the inventory you have left-over at the end of the month.

A simple Excel spreadsheet that lists all the things you sell in a category such as beverages (or tires, or men's clothing, or fishing gear), will have a place for you to input how many of these you have in inventory, how much each individual item costs you, a formula that multiplies the two and gives you a dollar value of what you have on hand. The spreadsheet will do this for each one of these and then add them all together so that you know how much of this one category you have on hand. It will look something like this.

Hand Count	MERCHANDISE	Amount	Price	Total
_____	Tee Shirt-Mens	46	8.75	402.5
_____	Sweatshirt	10	17.35	173.5
_____	Hat	1	6	6
_____	Mao Hat	8	10.25	82
_____	Frankenbrew	0	13.5	0
_____	Womens Tanks	45	9.75	438.75
_____	Long Sleeve Tees-Men	41	12.5	512.5
_____	Womens Long Sleeve	5	12.6	63
_____	Womens Cadet Jacket	12	18	216
_____	K.SM. Womens hats	0	8.19	0
_____	K. Mao Hats	6	8.19	49.14
_____	K. Mens hats	11	8.19	90.09
_____	LOGO Glasses	86	2.69	231.34
_____	Long Sleeve Hoodies	2	17.5	35
_____		0	0	0
_____		0	0	0
_____		0	0	0
_____		0	0	0
			$	2,299.82

Note the space on the left is where you can physically write down what you count when doing an inventory.

The next step in the inventory process is to figure out the cost of what you sold compared to the sales you brought in as a percentage. The basic formula to calculate that is:

Beginning Inventory + Purchases - Ending Inventory divided by Sales

Let me explain that. Going back to the Mexican Coke example, let's say you start the month out with 12 cokes. During the month you buy 24 more. When you do inventory at the end of the month you have 3.

How many did you sell? Well, 12 +24-3=33. So, you know how many you started the month out with because it was what you finished the previous month with, or last months ending inventory is this months beginning inventory. You also bought 24 more during the month. That means you had at least 36 (the 12 you started out with plus the 24 you bought) that you could sell. But when you took inventory at the end of the month, there was only three left. That must mean that hopefully you sold the difference, which is 33. Incidentally, that ending inventory of 3, is now your beginning inventory for the next month.

Looking at the inventory sheet on the previous page, you can see all the different things that were counted and multiplied against what they cost individually, to arrive at a total for all the merchandise you have on hand at the end of the month.

Plugging these numbers into the formula we just used but on the same spreadsheet would look like this.

	Merchandise
Beginning Inventory	1607.96
Purchases	1,200
Ending Inventory	$ 2,299.82
Cost of Goods Sold	$ 508.14
Sales	1987.98
PC	25.6%

PC is Product Cost as a %

There's a point to all of this. To know the second most important thing on our scoreboard, we need to know how to manage our cost of sales. To do that we need to be taking inventory and establishing target % for the items we sell.

Let's go back to the Mexican Coke example again. As you saw there were only 3 left when we took inventory at the end of the month, which would mean that we should have sold 33. But what if we only generated enough sales for 25 of them? What happened to the 8 others? They could have been broken, stolen, or not charged for. We wouldn't know that unless we did this inventory so we could catch the problem. See?

Whatever business you are in, you are selling something. To accurately keep track of the costs, you need to be comparing apples to apples. For example, if you had a sporting goods store it would be more accurate to track sales depending on what category. You wouldn't want to lump electronics like GPS and Watches in with Clothing. The markups would be different and depending on the sales mix it would tend to skew the cost percentages. It would be better to divide sales items up into categories like Electronics, Clothing, Sports Equipment and so on. When you did an inventory on these items, each category would have its own inventory sheet.

The way restaurants work is similar. You sell food, but you also sell wine, beer, spirits, and non-alcoholic beverages. You might also sell merchandise as well. Each one has a target cost percentage.

Food might be 25%, Wine 35%, Spirits 22%, Beer 30%, Non-Alcoholic Beverages 18%, and Merchandise 45%. Each one of these items would have its own inventory sheet. This sounds like a lot of inventories so you might want to assign one or two of each of these to different management positions. Here the kitchen manager would do Food, the bar manager would do Beer, Spirits and Wine and a shift manager could do Merchandise and Non-Alcoholic Beverages.

When you are planning out your business and what you want to sell, if you have done a business plan you must have projected what your costs would be. Those costs would be your target.

For a brewpub that I owned I established the following costs:

Food - 25%

Beer - 12% (less because we make it ourselves)

Wine - 38%

Beverages - 25%

Merchandise - 50%

In my projections, these are the numbers I used to see what my breakeven would be so naturally these are also my targets.

When I make my Scoreboard remember that the first item was:

Scoreboard

November

Sales Budget _$70,000_

Sales Pace   -_$69,783_

Now I'll add my cost of sales targets, which will look like this:

Food (25%) _____

Beer (12%) _____

Wine (38%) _____

Bev. (25%) _____

Merch. (50%) _____

When just starting out it is vital that you take an **inventory of everything you intend to sell before you open the doors for the first time.** What you need to do is establish a beginning inventory. It doesn't matter if you start your business on the 1st of the month or the 12th, what matters is that you know the dollar value of all the categories you set up to track.

Let's say you planned on opening on the 12th of the month, so the day before you did an inventory and ran the numbers through your inventory spreadsheets. That gives you your beginning inventories.

At the end of that first month, you will do an inventory again - this is done after close of business on the last day of the month and before you open again on the first day of the next month.

On your spreadsheets you take what you have as an ending inventory for the inventory you did on the 12th and move that number to the beginning inventory on this sheet you are filling at the end of the month. That's because at the end of the month you will have a new ending inventory. When you plug the numbers into your inventory sheet it will give you this.

Next you will add up what you purchased in this category and put that number in the space called purchases. Maybe you didn't purchase any new inventory so you would simply write in 0. Incidentally, if you are using a program like QuickBooks, every time you purchase something you assign a category to that purchase. So, if you bought something that was a cost of sale, like Food or Merchandise, QuickBooks will keep track of those purchases, so you simply run a report at the end of the month to get this purchase figure.

For Sales, your Point of Sales System (POS) will give you a report. Again, if you set up your POS for sales, you will want to categorize the sales to reflect your inventories. There won't be just one sales figure, but instead it will break the sales down as in our example, Food, Beer, Wine, Beverages, Merchandise. You just input these sales figures into your inventory sheets.

The inventories you just took will give you your current cost percentages. You write these percentages onto your scoreboard in the spaces next to the category shown. If your inventory percent hits your target or below, you write the percent in black. If the percent is higher than your target, write it in red. Black is good, Red is bad.

Food (25%) ___*24.2%*___

Beer (12%) ___ *11.8%*___

Wine (38%) ___*36.5%*___

Bev. (25%) ___*24.9%*___

Merch. (50%) _-*53.5%*___

Just with a glance you can see there is a problem. It could be that you miscounted on your inventory sheet, or it could be someone walked off with a hat. At least with this information you can try to locate the problem and come up with a better solution so that it won't happen again.

Once you believe you have found what the problem was, retake that one inventory to see if the percentage has come back down. If it has, put the new number in that space. Your goal is all the numbers in the black!

Labor Bank

Finally, we come to the last piece of the Scoreboard and the second biggest expense behind Cost of Sales.

As you saw, Sales Pace can change every day. The Cost of Sales, once you have done your inventories and your cost percentages are all in the black, you don't need to worry about that until the next inventory. So, you won't be changing those numbers daily.

But Labor, like sales will change every day, unless all your staff is on salary (if everyone was on salary, your daily labor wouldn't change because the salaries are fixed, and you know what they are everyday). In most small businesses however, most employees are on hourly.

There are different ways you can figure out your labor budgets. A typical way is to have a target percent of sales. For example, if I had a sales budget for the month set at $70,000 and I had a target labor percent of 28%, then I know I could spend $19,600 for the month.

If my store was open 31 days, then my daily labor budget would be $632.25 ($19,600 divided by 31). That's simple enough and you might want to try that.

For me however, I like to be more precise in my labor estimates. That's because you need a certain number of staff no matter what the sales are. You can try to cut it down or beef it up but tying your cost of labor as a percent of sales doesn't always work.

If I calculated what my labor would be by calculating my labor needs, I simply make up a month schedule showing each position, how many hours they worked per day times what their hourly pay was. This would give me my total for the month and that total I would divide by how many days I was open, which would give me my daily labor dollars I could spend.

Why Call It a Bank?

The best way to think of the Labor Bank is to see it as though every day you deposited your budget ($632.25) into this account, and every day you wrote a check out of it to pay for labor. Since you probably will have labor that is higher or lower each day than your projections, there will either be a deficit or a positive number in this account. Like a bank account this gets accumulated.

Let's say on day one you spend $630.99. This is just what your POS (point of sales) shows because it is the device your employees use to clock in and clock out. Maybe someone clocked out a little early, which is why the daily labor is less than you projected.

On your labor bank page, you would write - in black because this number is positive - $1.26. Excellent, you are in positive territory.

However, the next day is a Friday and very busy. You had to keep your help on a little extra to handle the sales volume. You spend $662.85.

To calculate this into your Labor Bank you need to take that day's deposit of $632.25, plus $1.26 (what you had left over from the day before) minus what you just spent $662.85 to get your new Labor Bank Total, 632.25+1.26-662.85=29.34. This number now is written down in your labor bank.

Labor Bank (*$632.25*) -*$29.34*

Remember the next day you get another $632.25, so theoretically you can try to get some employees clocked out a little early to try to make up for this $29.34 deficit. Of course, Saturday could be busy too, but that's OK. Come Monday it will be slower, and you can cut on staff, probably through Thursday and get enough ahead in your daily labor bank to cover a busy weekend coming up!

The End Result

This is what your scoreboard looks like now.

Scoreboard

November

Sales Budget *$70,000*

Sales Pace *$69,783*

Food (25%) *24.2%*

Beer (12%) *11.8%*

Wine (38%) *36.5%*

Bev. (25%) *24.9%*

Merch. (50%) *53.5%*

Labor Bank (*$632.25*) -*$29.34*

So, what does this do for you? Well, we said using the Pareto Principal that we wanted to concentrate on the 20% of our efforts that provides 80% of our results. That we figure comes down to Sales, Cost of Sales, and Labor.

In other words, if I only had 30 minutes extra per week that I could spend on business development, I could spend it trying to find a cheaper plastic trash bag or sitting down and figuring out a new sales promotion. Which do you think would be time better spent?

With a scoreboard, you know that if everything is in the black, you are going to have a profitable month. You know this everyday too because you are monitoring these vitals in real time.

Let's say you get 2 days off, and I hope you do, and you come back from your weekend camping with the family. You walk into the office and take one look at the scoreboard that the shift managers have kept current, and you know in 2 seconds if your business is OK or not. If everything is Black, then you are fine. If for some reason you come in for your shift and everything is black except for Labor, which is $29.34 in the red, then armed with this information on your shift you can try to get someone off the clock a little earlier to start to make up for that negative number.

If the Sales Budget is supposed to be $70,000, but it is in the red showing $69,783, you can try to think of something you could do to increase sales. For example, you could look at similar stores to yours but in a different city and state. Look at their web site and see what they are doing. There might be some great sales idea they use that you could introduce into your store.

The scoreboard is the ultimate tool to the business system that will start paying you dividends on day one. As I mentioned before, you can reach out to me and I can send you a Daily Sales Report (DSR) that calculates Sales pace and daily labor for you, so it doesn't take any extra time every day. No strings attached.

Why am I so stoked on the scoreboard? It is your business ***Superpower!*** This tool, that doesn't even take 5 minutes a day to fill out, will keep you on top of the 20% that gives you 80% every single day of the year. At the end of that year, you will be in a much better place than had you not followed this simple system. Pareto would approve.

Step 11
Action Item

- Buy a Dry Erase board and a red and black dry erase marker

- Write at the top Scoreboard and the month

- Write Sales Budget $70,000

- Every day write in Sales Pace $69,783

- List the categories of what you sell with their target cost percent next to each, followed by the current cost percent. Merch. (45%) 44.3%

- Write Labor Bank with your daily labor budget next to it and your labor bank balance next to that every day. Labor Bank ($632.25) -$29.34

- Budget met = Write in Black

- Budget not met = Write in Red

STEP 11:

Your Oyster

Many years ago, my partners and I would go on fishing expeditions. Not for fish, but for ideas. Being in the restaurant business we wanted to go to creative food markets to see how other people were doing their restaurants. Most of the time we went to San Francisco, which at the time was the epicenter of what was then being called "New American Cuisine". Most things were viewed as cutting edge and an excellent place to get ideas.

We would visit at least 20 restaurants per day - no kidding! - and glean what we could. Some we just popped in to have a look, some we would get an appetizer or a drink, others a full meal. We weren't trying to steal concepts, just small things that we could bring home to our restaurants and keep them interesting. It could be the menu design, or the way the table was set, or even food ideas. We always came away with something.

Once we were there and bored of fine dining and wound up in a small pizzeria. It was different than most we had been to in the past. It was more interesting architecturally and the menu had more interesting ingredients. What we liked about it also was the fact that it wasn't full service. When your order was ready, they called your name, and you went up to the counter to pick up your pizza.

Back home in Albuquerque there was a restaurant by the university called Frontier Cafe - it's still there - and they had the same type of service where you ordered at the counter, and they called your name when it was ready.

At the time we were operating a full-on Italian Restaurant called Scalo. We had 100 employees, white table clothes and it was really a great restaurant. We owned it for 30 years. Anyway, we thought, what if you took a pizza concept but put it in a nice upscale atmosphere, but still had counter service. Also keep the prices really affordable and by using a traditional wood fired oven, the food could be made super-fast. We didn't know it at the time, but we invented a concept called Fast Casual. This was 1991.

But getting back to the look of the place. We wanted it to have a certain vibe. We were at another restaurant in San Francisco called the Balboa Cafe - it's still there too - and it had a vibe that really felt good. I met the owner and commented on it to him. He said it was his Oyster.

What he meant by Oyster, was the feeling or the vibe of the restaurant that was a self-contained world within its shell, like an oyster. It was their job to manage that vibe.

When we got back from that trip with visions of a pizzeria in our future, we would set up Scalo every day and ask how the Oyster was. We had no definition for it, but we understood generally what it meant.

As the years went by however, I felt that a real definition was needed because it was becoming an integrated part of our business and as we grew, we wanted to teach managers this concept as well.

Now I feel it is one of the most important things in a business system that you can have and why I want to include it here.

Review

So far in our business system build, we have:

- Identified the positions in or business
- Made training checklists for each of those positions
- Made daily checklists for employees to follow in those positions
- Added weekly side-work to the daily checklists
- Created a GM book to catch tasks that are only done every so often
- Made internal audits so that the managers can make sure everyone is doing their checklists
- Created an External audit completed by someone outside the business to make sure the managers are doing their checklists
- Conduct a weekly manager meeting to keep up with changes to the business and keep everything fresh
- Create a Scoreboard so that you can track Sales, Cost of Sales, and Labor on a daily basis.

While this is a very good operating system for your business, it's time to cap it off with the finishing touch that doesn't cost anything but will give you a truly competitive advantage.

If you deal with customers at all in person, understanding your oyster will go a long way to make doing business with you a pleasurable experience.

Many large national brands understand this. Starbucks has a look and feel. J. Crew has it too. Whole Foods understands this and so does MUJI in Portland, that sells specialty interior decorating items.

Any serious professional retail establishment has a "look". They might not call it an Oyster, but it's the same thing. These places recognize the importance of an atmosphere that emphasizes their brand.

The only difference between these super cool national brands and your business is that they recognize this and manage it, while small mom and pop places don't.

When I began to define what I felt the Oyster was, I divided it into 5 things:

- Music
- Lighting
- Temperature
- Cleanliness
- Stage Setting

Really, none of these things will cost you anything extra, but knowing how this works is an integral part of your business system. So, let's break it down.

Music

I can't think of a retail space that wouldn't benefit from some sort of background music. It fills the dead spaces and gives the shopper a feeling of activity.

There are two parts to music. Volume and type.

Volume

Basically, the volume of the music should be at your normal speaking volume. While the music is playing you can still have a casual conversation without someone over-hearing you.

There are exceptions to this of course. When you first open your doors for the day, you might want to turn the volume up, just a bit. This will help fill in the dead spaces because your store or restaurant is empty. When customers come in, they will get a sense of energy from the music, and it makes their entry into your business more seamless and less intrusive. However, once you have customers in, then it's time to turn the music back down to its set-point. If the music remains too loud, then the customers have a hard time hearing your salesclerks or wait staff, or each other for that matter.

On the other hand, if the music is too low, a customer's voice or your own will go lower to compensate. This gives a feeling of discomfort.

We teach a class on how to open a brewery and when I explain this concept to the students, it's usually at lunch in our brewpub. I can control the volume and type of music with my phone, so while we are talking, I will slowly lower the volume of the music. You can actually "feel" the energy drain from the room and the conversations from the other customers start to lower volume almost to a whisper.

If on the other hand I start raising the volume in a full dining room, the sound level from the music and the elevated voices becomes uncomfortable.

Play around with this and see what works for you. I find the Sonos speakers give a full rich sound and operate through your phone.

One thing to be aware of is if you are playing music for your customers you need to be paying for a service that covers copywrite fees to the artists. There are plenty of services that do this, and a simple Google search will allow you to compare prices and programs.

There are a couple ways around paying for a service also. One is to simply play the radio. The problem with that is you are also playing commercials. The other way is to play music in which you have permission from the artist. But keep it simple, just sign on to a service and your life will be easier.

Type of Music

The other aspect of music is what kind you want to play. I would be surprised if small operations put much thought into this. However, the type of music you play is as important as any other part of the oyster. The type of music you play will set the mood of your business, but it's not simply plug and play. Like other aspects of the Oyster, the type of music you choose is very nuanced.

First, who are your clientele? Are they hipsters or retired baby boomers? Do you have tourists coming from all over the US, or are you next to a college?

Also, the time of day, the season you are in, and the weather. I wouldn't pick reggae music on a cold rainy day. But some Dave Brubeck would feel just right.

Can you imagine a golf shop in a retirement community in Florida playing thrasher music? Can you imagine a brewpub next to a university playing Mozart? How about a Chinese restaurant playing Mariachi? These might be extreme examples, but they do show how some thought must go into your choice of music.

The worst thing you can do is to let the bartender, salesclerks, legal secretary, or just anyone in your establishment pick out whatever they want.

In our first restaurant, and this goes way back, we made cassette tapes to play. Our restaurant was only open for lunch and happy hour, and we were in a large building in downtown Albuquerque that had the biggest bank in New Mexico, and the two largest law firms as well in the building. That was the bulk of our customers.

To make music back then - way before we were even aware of the Oyster - we made these tapes and labelled them Lunch Jazz One, followed by Lunch Jazz Two and so on. We thought it would give an air of sophistication to our little lunch spot, and it did.

There are music services you can subscribe to that will not only pay your music royalty fees but give you a selection of music that will fit the mood you are trying to achieve in your store. That's the easiest solution. I know from experience that if you let your employees pick the music out, you will not be happy with the effect it has on your idea of what your business feels like to the customers.

Lighting

I would guess that many small shop owners don't give much thought to lighting. When they acquired their space, the lighting was already in place and if it all worked and was adequate, they didn't worry about it.

Lighting, however, plays a big part in the atmosphere you are trying to achieve. For example, can you imagine instead of the nice lamps in your home you had a bunch of canned fluorescent lights in your ceiling? It wouldn't feel very cozy, would it? In fact, it would be simply depressing. So why on earth would you subject your customers to this?

My **first rule** of lighting in a space that serves customers is *No Fluorescent lights!*

These lights in most cases wash out color from everything they illuminate. Especially skin tones, leaving people looking sick. Of course, there are soft fluorescents and Whole Foods Market makes good use of them.

However, the other reason I don't like them is because you can't dim them. I'm talking about those long 4-foot and 8-foot fluorescent lights. I will say technology is changing and some you can dim, but overall, they are still boring to look at.

So instead, pick lighting that is warm and dimmable. This is important because as a rule in lighting, you want it to reflect what the natural light isn't doing outside. If the sun is bright, you want the lights to be bright inside to balance the outside light coming in from your windows. If you do not, then your retail space will feel like a cave.

As the sun goes down, so does your interior light, to a point. The best way to figure out what that point is to be in your store or restaurant, or office when you are closed at night and play with the dimmer switch. Adjust the lights down until everything feels warm and inviting, while still providing enough light to see what you are selling. You've seen those restaurants where the lighting at night is so low that the patrons are moving the candle closer to their menus or turning on their phone flashlights to see.

When you have found what you believe to be the perfect lighting for your store, take a permanent marker and mark the spot on the dimmer switch. That way as the seasons change and you are adjusting the lights down to its low point, you won't go below where you had figured the perfect spot to be. This is a nice low-tech solution.

My **second rule** for lighting is *Be Creative in your Fixtures!*

Why have boring lights when for not much money you can do something unique. All it takes is a little imagination, or a little thievery.

By thievery I mean wherever you go in your travels, look at lights that you find interesting. You can probably re-create it in your shop for very little money.

There are plenty of specialty light stores that will sell you some really cool light fixtures for a whole lot of money. But then I go back to a small coffeehouse in Lauterbrunnen, Switzerland. Listen, I've been to a thousand coffeehouses but here is the reason I remember this one. It was the light fixtures over the tables.

They consisted of a green-glass mason jar with blue aquarium gravel in the bottom. Sitting on top of the gravel was a little yellow rubber duck. The light bulb was above that. The cost to make that fixture? Probably less than $30. It gave off a nice light with the combination of colors, but more importantly it was unique. So much so that I remember it all these years later, which means I remember the coffeehouse too. Wouldn't you like something like that in your place?

Here are some things I've seen that stick out.

- Sail Lights. Basically, just a light bulb hanging down but shading it a white piece of fiberglass paper with two willow sticks holding the sides. The "sail" was suspended from the ceiling by 4 lengths of invisible fishing line. As air moved through the space from the heater or air conditioner, the sail moved gently in the air.

- Cheese Grater Sconces. With light bulbs coming out of the wall, they were shaded with chrome cheese graters. The little holes in the cheese graters diffused the light along the wall.

- A chandelier made of an old, weathered door and hanging from the door was a collection of pendant lights of all shapes, sizes, and lengths.

- A mishmash of bicycle wheels with lights intertwined hanging from the ceiling.

You get the idea. Really, just about anything you can think of. Even if your lights cost a bit more, this is one thing that will stick out with your customers, and they will remember you for it. Even if it is just a rubber duck in a glass jar that makes you ask "why?".

Temperature

Temperature in your shop might be something you never thought about, but it should be. Especially if you have a kind of business where customers will be in there for a while. That includes bars and restaurants, movie theaters, bowling alleys, hair salons, doctors, and dentist offices. If a customer is going to be in your establishment for more than 15 minutes, you really must key into the Oyster here.

Think about it. Have you ever noticed in hot climates like in Florida or Phoenix, that people going into a restaurant will be bringing their sweaters? It's because the air conditioner is going to be cranked way down. And the reason for this is because the staff is running around, and they are hot. So, they are setting the air conditioner to suit themselves. Same goes for winter in cold climates, The heat will be low to compensate for the employees working up a sweat.

It's not just restaurants but shopping malls, movies theaters, and even office buildings.

If your customers are coming into your business in the Winter and they will be there a while, watch to see if they take their coats off. Same goes for in the summer if your regulars are coming in with sweaters when it's 90 degrees outside, you've got a problem.

The best way to deal with temperature is to watch your customers. If they never take their coats off, then they are not comfortable, so why would they come back when there are other more relaxing places to go?

This is such a simple thing to deal with and should be obvious. You could lock your thermostat so it can't be changed but just like in the rest of the Oyster, it needs to be managed.

Where I live in Colorado it can be very hot in the summer, but an afternoon thunderstorm can drop the temperature 30 degrees in less than 5 minutes. You want to be able to make the changes quickly.

Our little brewpub in Ridgway, Colorado has a front door that is 4 foot wide. There is no vestibule on this historic building, so every time the front door is opened during the winter months, a blast of cold air swoops in and right on a row of tables.

To combat this, just to the right of the front door on the inside, is the brewhouse with the kettle being closest to the front door. I would fill the kettle with water and fire it up before opening, then turn it off right as we opened at 4:00. I would lift the lid to the kettle to let the steam out and this would help heat the entry way.

My goal if it was cold and snowy outside was to give the customer who walked in the door a feeling like a set of warm open arms enveloped the customers in a welcome hug. It works, but some sort of vestibule still needs to be made.

The other night we went into a popular restaurant on our way home from shopping. We were there just after the rush, and it was cool outside. The first thing I notices was a ceiling fan right above the host stand blowing cool air down in the entry full force. It was not a welcoming feeling. The next thing I noticed was the lights were on too bright. This also detracted from the feeling of warmth. Once seated I also notice it was simply cool in the dining room. This was November in Colorado. I could see other customers still had their jackets on and I wasn't about to take mine off. I did see however the staff just wearing their tee shirts and were very comfortable as they were in constant motion.

The food was great, and the prices were fine, but I would think twice about going back next time.

Most things that experts suggest to better your business require big changes and big bucks. With managing the oyster, it only costs you being aware. It's not too difficult to put yourself in the shoes of a customer. Turn the fans off when it's cool outside. Turn the lights down as it starts to get dark in the evening and set your thermostat to a comfortable temperature that suits your customers, not your staff.

The last thing I also noticed when we arrived after the rush was the tables were still a mess and it took a while to get things organized again, which brings me to the next part of the Oyster.

Cleanliness

This should almost go without saying, but your business not only needs to be clean, but it should feel organized too. This is not something that is going to register with your customers in a conscious way, but it will get noticed.

You know what it is like when you are home and the dishes are done, the bed is made, and the house is clean. It simply feels better. Compared to a sink full of dirty dishes, messy bed, and clothes lying on the floor. You are not the only one. Your customers feel this too, so when your business is tidy, the customer just feels better, which is the heart of the whole Oyster concept.

There are two parts to this.

Physically Clean

In the system that you have built with your checklists you now have a way of keeping everything in your business looking clean and in good repair.

Any business will start to wear-out after time because of the constant use by thousands of customers over the years. But with your checklist system and using the GM book you can keep all the dust balls and chipped paint taken care of.

Your outside audits will give you a customer perspective if your auditor doesn't work for you and comes into your business with a fresh set of eyes. You put a lot of work into your business to make it have a certain curb-appeal, and it works. Your customers are not only noticing what you sell, but also the look of your place as well, and they will notice the dust balls that you simply cannot see because you are in there day after day.

Being in the restaurant business for so long, I notice customers when they are sitting at their table really look around. They even look up at the walls and the ceiling because the restaurant has been decorated so well, it's almost like a theater. They want to admire it, so they notice the vent at the top of the wall that is growing fur. You the owner without the audit system will never look up and see that. It may seem like a small thing, but it is all part of the package.

It's not like the customer will walk away and think, "that was such a clean place". But it will make an impression. On the other hand, if it is dirty, they may easily walk away telling their friends that the place was like a pit. Just look up restaurant reviews on Google and you will have your proof.

Organized

It's one thing to be clean but you also need to be organized. Customers do not treat your business like they do their own homes (well actually they might).

At a restaurant they will spill food on the floor, drinks on the table, spill salt and sugar and generally make a mess. Especially if they have kids with them. Once they leave the staff must get that cleaned up as fast as possible, but also put the table back together to its original set-point.

By set-point I mean how a table is supposed to look. You choreograph the table-top in how you place the salt and pepper shakers, napkin and silverware and anything else you have on the table. Every table should be the same and the chairs cleaned off and pushed back to the table. This communicates to the customer that it is ready to be seated. If the chairs were left out at odd angles and the condiments on the table-top left in disarray, the customer isn't sure that they should sit there or not.

In a retail store, customers are pulling clothes off the racks, trying them on or just looking closer at them, then either putting the clothes back on the rack or simply laying them down in a crumpled mess on a counter. It is the clerk's responsibility to refold or hang the sweater and place it on the rack where it belongs as though new, and the previous customer hasn't touched it.

The same is true for products on the shelves. You need to constantly go around the store and pull products forward if there is a gap where a customer has bought something. Not only do you bring forward the products from the back to fill that empty space, but you should also face all the labels forward in a uniform manner. This is a good thing to do during down times as well.

In the meantime, you are constantly picking up any trash that is on the floor, cleaning the smudge marks on the glass counter tops and keeping everything in order.

Even an office needs to be organized. If there is a waiting room, you want the magazines to be arranged on the table, so it doesn't look messy. The restrooms need to be wiped down often during the day and to make sure the customer who washes their hands has a clean towel to dry them on. That's the worst if the towel dispenser is empty and it isn't discovered until a customer has dripping hands and no place to dry them.

In the office you want to keep the coffee fresh if offered, and the candy bowl full. In other words, the reception area should look as good at 2 in the afternoon as it does at 9 in the morning.

Cleanliness is such an old-fashioned notion, but it is a vital part of the Oyster. As I mentioned, your customers are only going to remark on this if your business isn't clean or organized. If it is, they will notice it on a subconscious level, but still a very real and good feeling. They might not be able to put a finger on it, but they just feel comfortable in your business and are likely to return.

Stage Setting

This is my favorite part of the oyster, and the most important part. I like to call it a stage setting, because to me, a business is much like a play. It certainly is a performance where you have your stage where the actors (your staff) perform their rehearsed roles and the customers (theater goers) pay you.

Elevator Speech

If we were introduced by a mutual friend and you said you had a business, and I were to ask you what kind of business, could you answer me with a sentence or two?

If you could, you have the makings of your Stage Setting. If you can't, then you may be unclear about what the look and feel of your business is about.

If you told me, you owned a Slam-Poetry Coffee House, boy I think I know exactly what that coffee house looks like, what kind of music is being played, what the baristas look like and the general vibe. And you told me all that with one sentence.

Or I run a Wilderness Fly Fishing Expedition Outfitter Store. Again, I think I would have a pretty good feel for what that would look like and what kind of fly-fishing gear you would be selling. I can picture also vintage rods and reels on the walls with wood fishing nets, maybe some great photos of fisherman out in the mountains. Maybe a huge map of Alaska and the great Salmon fishing there.

On the other hand, if someone said she ran a woman's shoe store and that was all she said, I would have no idea what that shoe store was like. If she said however, that she ran an affordable women's shoe store called Two Feet In Heaven, I can picture rows and rows of fun and interesting shoes in a very light-hearted atmosphere.

So, to begin the process it is vital that you think how you could describe your business in as few words as possible. Because the clearer you are on your concept, the easier it is to describe it. You may have never thought of this before: you are just opening a shoe store. But if you can pick a theme or idea that drives your business, it not only focuses what you plan to do, but how you will do it. This is big stuff. It can't just be a store or a restaurant you are opening. There is more to opening a real estate office other than just selling real estate. Why have just another doctor's office? What you are doing is based on your personality and your interests. We are all different and unique in our own way.

Your shoe store reflects the kind of shoes you like and how they make you feel. Your restaurant is not just an Italian restaurant but reflects the great time you had eating at restaurants in Northern Italy, and you want to recreate the nuanced feeling of those trattoria's.

Anyone can sell real estate, but what if your office was more like a comfortable home, where you could offer your clients a great cup of coffee, or even a glass of wine or beer? That sounds much better than a strip-mall office space with white walls and plastic furniture.

You see, by thinking about how to define your stage setting, you will naturally take that setting and work its way through all the other aspects of your oyster.

If your fly-fishing shop is geared to the adventurous fly fisher, then how can you reflect that in the types of lighting you have. Can you make lights out of fly rods? What type of music fits in with this vibe? What is the person at the counter going to be wearing?

When we opened our first big restaurant, we were inspired by the Italian trattoria's we had seen in Italy. They had an old-world charm and a casualness in their service. The kitchen wasn't in the back, but right out front where the customers could see what was going on. Also, we didn't want people to think we would be just another Italian restaurant with a candle stuck in a Chianti bottle on a red checkered tablecloth. We called our restaurant a Northern Italian Grill, which we thought would make customers believe it would be different. This was in 1987, and the concept was very different back then - not so much now.

With that picture in mind, we completely opened the kitchen to the dining room, and then built up the seating so that it felt like the kitchen was a stage and the tables were the audience.

The wait staff dressed in white shirts, black pants, real black bow ties that they had to learn how to tie, and long white bistro aprons that went all the way to the ground. The tables had white table clothes but white butcher paper on top of that. While this all looked very fancy, we went out of our way to make the menu very affordable.

All these things were put into place because we had a clear vision of how we wanted to set the stage. The colors on the walls, the artwork, the light fixtures all fit into this. Even Italian Language instruction piped into the restrooms.

The steps we took in a simple Italian restaurant, work in basically any business where a customer walks in the door. Once you know what your business is about, then you go back to the other steps of the Oyster and integrate those Stage Setting adjustments into each one of the steps. It pulls it altogether.

The Oyster, as I've said, doesn't really cost you anything. It simply takes being aware of the five parts and implementing them. I can't overstate the effect this will have on your business enough.

I had a friend who opened a real estate office in another Colorado town I used to live in. He and his wife were very aware of the Oyster, and we talked about it quite a bit. When they opened their office, they decided to jump on board with the Oyster concept and implement it into everything.

Until then, the established real estate offices were the typical ones you would find in a strip center or a converted house. The walls were painted white, the furniture was cheap, the lighting was office fluorescent.

My friends recognized that a home purchase is in most cases the largest purchase someone will ever make. In addition, real estate prices were climbing rapidly in the town and most of the shoppers were higher end purchasers.

To attract these, and any potential home buyers, they wanted their office to reflect the tastes of the fine homes that people were interested in purchasing. They had a vision that when a customer came in the door, they would be comfortable to the point of wanting to "hang out" in the office, rather than just conduct business. Basically, they wanted their office to look like a nice home.

So, they decorated it with soft colors on the walls, real art and not that type of art that is in banks and hotel rooms. The furniture was expensive and comfortable. Fresh flowers were on the table and brochures of properties featured were displayed on a coffee table. If the receptionist served you a cup of coffee or tea, it was served in a real cup, rather than a paper one. There was music too, just in the background, but still audible and typically jazz standards from the '50's.

Almost from the very beginning their real estate company dominated the market. The reason is simple. If you are going to spend all that money for a home, you want to do it with someone who understands the magnitude of the purchase and makes you feel special.

The investment in the Oyster was minimal for my friends, but the payoff was off the charts.

Understanding and implementing the Oyster in your business will be a game-changing experience. You have absolutely nothing to lose in trying it, and certainly everything to gain.

Large national brands know all too well the importance of the Oyster, though they don't call it that. Now with knowledgeable eyes, when you go into an office, retail store, or restaurant, check out their oyster. If it is a chain, their Oyster, or vibe is no accident. See what they did and try to figure out why they decorated the way they do. It's all part of a plan.

It works for the national brands. It will work for you too.

Step 11
Action Item

- **Music** - volume should be at your normal speaking level, not too low, which makes people want to whisper, and not too loud, which gives customers a headache

- **Music** - Pick what fits with your customers, not what your employees want to hear.

- **Lighting** - No white florescent lights. Lights should be warm and dimmable. Be creative with your fixtures.

- **Lighting** - When it's bright outside, your lights should be bright inside to balance the light with the outside. However, as the sun goes down, the lights inside should too until it reaches that sweet spot where the space feels warm and comfortable, but the customer can still see.

- **Temperature** - Watch your customers to see if they look comfortable. If they don't take off their coats, they are cold. Too often the temperature is set for the employees rather than the customers. Be aware of the customers body language.

- **Cleanliness** - Not only should your space be clean and in good repair, but it should have an orderliness to it, as though you choreographed the space.

- **Stage Setting** - See if you can describe your business in one or two sentences. Once you can do that, set the stage, or the look of your business in line with how you described it. This will make your business feel more cohesive.

CONCLUSION

Great businesses don't just happen. They start with a vision of the entrepreneur who created it. This vision is important in getting a business off the ground, but it is sadly deficient when it comes to making a business survive for the long haul.

This is where a business system comes into play. This little book has been a battle plan for the growth and survival of your business.

But before you put this book away, let me remind you of our friend Vilfredo Pareto. Remember, he said that 80% of your results come from 20% of your efforts. Doing the 12 steps plus the Scoreboard and Oyster is your 20%.

Think of the amount of work that went into opening the doors of your business. Probably years of thinking about it, planning and saving to get to the starting line.

If you compare that amount of effort to doing these steps, it's like a ripple in the ocean. Find the energy over the next couple days to get a rough draft of these steps down on paper. You can rewrite them as your business grows.

With a business operation structure as part of your business, you not only get to the starting blocks, but you now have a way to keep on the track.